Ready for an adventure? This neckwear collection is teeming with textures and color schemes to inspire your knitting creativity. For beginners to intermediate knitters, nine designs feature diverse yarns ranging from super fine weight to bulky. Enjoy the variety!

LEISURE ARTS, INC.
Maumelle, Arkansas

Geometric Striped Cowl

SHOPPING LIST

Yarn (Light Weight) 🧶3

- ☐ Color A (Brown)- 40 yards
  (36.5 meters)
- ☐ Color B (Salmon) - 40 yards
  (36.5 meters)
- ☐ Color C (Ecru) - 40 yards
  (36.5 meters)

Knitting Needle

- ☐ 24" (61 cm) Circular,
  size 8 (5 mm)
  or size needed for gauge

Additional Supplies

- ☐ Yarn needle

Finished Size: 23" circumference x 5" high (58.5 cm x 12.5 cm)

GAUGE INFORMATION

In Garter Stitch,
   17 sts and 34 rows = 4"
   (10 cm)

TECHNIQUES USED

• Adding stitches (*Figs. 2a & b,
   page 42*)
• K2 tog (*Fig. 5, page 43*)

BOTTOM SECTION

With Color A, cast on 100 sts;
do **not** join.

Row 1: Knit across.

Carry unused color along edge.

Rows 2-15: Knit across working in the following stripe sequence: 2 Rows **each** of Color B, ★ Color C, Color A, Color B; repeat from ★ once **more**.

Cut Color A and Color C.

CENTER SECTION

Center is worked across 7 new stitches, knitting last stitch together with next stitch on Bottom Section.

With Color B, add on 7 sts: 107 sts.

Row 1 (Right side)**:** K6, K2 tog; turn.

Row 2: Slip 1 as if to **knit**, K5, P1.

Rows 3-198: Repeat Rows 1 and 2 working in the following stripe sequence: 2 Rows **each**

of Color C, Color A, ★ Color B, Color C, Color A; repeat from ★ 31 times **more**: 8 sts.

Cut Color B and Color C.

Bind off all sts in **knit**.

TOP SECTION

With **right** side facing and Color B, pick up 100 sts across Center Section (**Fig. 8, page 45**).

Row 1: Knit across.

Rows 2-15: Knit across working in the following stripe sequence: 2 Rows **each** of Color A, ★ Color C, Color B, Color A; repeat from ★ once **more**.

Cut Color B and Color C.

Bind off all sts in **knit**.

Sew short edges together.

Garter Stripes Cowl

SHOPPING LIST

Yarn (Medium Weight) 4

- ☐ Color A (Ecru) - 110 yards (101 meters)
- ☐ Color B (Metallic) - 85 yards (77.5 meters)

Knitting Needles

- ☐ 24" (61 cm) Circular, size 9 (5.5 mm)
  or size needed for gauge
- ☐ Straight, size 8 (5 mm) (for Band)

Additional Supplies

- ☐ Stitch marker
- ☐ Yarn needle

Finished Size: 27" circumference x 6" high (68.5 cm x 15 cm)

GAUGE INFORMATION

With circular needle, in pattern,
  16 sts = 4" (10 cm)

COWL

With circular needle and Color A, cast on 108 sts; place marker to indicate beginning of rnd *(see Markers and Circular Knitting, page 41)*.

Carry unused color on **wrong** side.

Rnd 1 (Right side): With Color A, knit around.

Rnd 2: Purl around.

Rnds 3 and 4: With Color B, knit around.

Repeat Rnds 1-4 for pattern until Cowl measures approximately 6" (15 cm) from cast on edge, ending by working Rnd 2.

Bind off all sts, making sure the bind off is not too tight, as follows:

K3, ★ pass the the first st over 2 sts and off the right point, K1; repeat from ★ around until all of the sts on the left point have been used.
Pass the first st over 2 sts and off the right point, pass the second st over the third st and off the right point; cut yarn and pull end through remaining st.

BAND

With straight needles, Color B and leaving a long end for sewing, cast on 26 sts.

Rows 1-3: Knit across.

Row 4 (Wrong side)**:** Purl across.

Rows 5-18: Repeat Rows 1-4, 3 times; then repeat Rows 1 and 2 once **more**.

Bind off all sts in **knit**.

Wrap Band around Cowl and sew end of rows together.

Lace Cowl

SHOPPING LIST

Yarn (Fine Weight)

- ☐ 200 yards (183 meters)

Knitting Needle

- ☐ 24" (61 cm) Circular, size 10 (6 mm)
  or size needed for gauge

Additional Supplies

- ☐ Stitch marker

Finished Size: 28" circumference x 9" high (71 cm x 23 cm)

GAUGE INFORMATION

In Stockinette Stitch,
   14 sts and 22 rnds = 4"
   (10 cm)
In pattern,
   14 sts = 4¼" (10.75 cm)

TECHNIQUES USED

• YO *(Fig. 3a, page 42)*
• K2 tog *(Fig. 5, page 43)*

COWL

Cast on 92 sts; place marker to indicate beginning of rnd *(see Markers and Circular Knitting, page 41)*.

Rnds 1 and 2 (Right side)**:** (K2, P2) around.

Rnds 3-5: Knit around.

Rnd 6: (YO, K2 tog) around.

Rnds 7 and 8: Knit around.

Rnd 9: (K2 tog, YO) around.

Rnds 10-14: Knit around.

Repeat Rnds 6-14 for pattern until Cowl measures approximately 8¾" (22 cm) from cast on edge, ending by working Rnd 12.

Last 2 Rnds: (K2, P2) around.

Bind off all sts in pattern.

Mosaic Cowl

SHOPPING LIST
Yarn
(Super Fine Weight)
- ☐ Color A (Off White) - 90 yards (82.5 meters)
- ☐ Color B (Self-striping) - 65 yards (59.5 meters)

(Fine Weight)
- ☐ Color C (Fuchsia Metallic) - 50 yards (45.5 meters)

Knitting Needle
- ☐ 24" (61 cm) Circular, size 9 (5.5 mm) **or** size needed for gauge

Additional Supplies
- ☐ Yarn needle

Finished Size: 27" circumference x 7" high (68.5 cm x 18 cm)

GAUGE INFORMATION

In Stockinette Stitch,
    20 sts and 28 rows = 4"
    (10 cm)
In pattern,
    24 rows (2 repeats) = 2½"
    (6.25 cm)

COWL

When instructed to slip 2, always slip as if to **purl** with yarn on **wrong** side.

Carry unused color along edge.

With Color A, cast on 138 sts; do **not** join.

Rows 1 and 2: Knit across.

Row 3 (Right side)**:** With Color B, (K6, slip 2) across to last 2 sts, K2.

Row 4: P2, (slip 2, P6) across.

Rows 5 and 6: Repeat Rows 3 and 4.

Rows 7 and 8: With Color A, knit across.

Row 9: With Color C, K2, (slip 2, K6) across.

Row 10: (P6, slip 2) across to last 2 sts, P2.

Rows 11 and 12: Repeat Rows 9 and 10.

Rows 13-66: Repeat Rows 1-12, 4 times; then repeat Rows 1-6 once **more**.

Cut Color B and Color C.

Rows 67-69: With Color A, knit across.

Bind off all sts in **knit**.

Weave end of rows together *(Fig. 9, page 45)*.

Triangle Scarf

SHOPPING LIST

Yarn (Super Fine Weight)

☐ Color A (Blue) - 295 yards
  (270 meters)

☐ Color B (Ecru) - 210 yards
  (192 meters)

☐ Color C (Multi) - 250 yards
  (229 meters)

Knitting Needle

☐ 24" (61 cm) Circular, size 8 (5 mm)
  or size needed for gauge

Additional Supplies

☐ Stitch marker

Finished Size: 46" wide x 21" long (117 cm x 53.5 cm)

GAUGE INFORMATION

In Stockinette Stitch, holding
  2 strands of yarn together,
  18 sts and 32 rows = 4"
  (10 cm)

TECHNIQUES USED

• Knit increase *(Figs. 4a & b, page 43)*

Hold 2 strands of the same color yarn together throughout. Wind each color into 2 separate balls or use the yarn from the inside and the outside of the skein. Carry unused yarn along edge, twisting yarns every 4 rows.

SCARF

Holding 2 strands of Color A together, cast on 4 sts.

Row 1: Knit across.

Row 2 (Right side)**:** Knit increase twice, place marker *(see Markers, page 41)*, knit increase twice: 8 sts.

Row 3: Purl across.

Row 4 (Increase row)**:** Knit increase, knit across to within one st of marker, knit increase, slip marker, knit increase, knit across to last st, knit increase: 12 sts.

Row 5: Purl across.

Rows 6-9: Repeat Rows 4 and 5 twice: 20 sts.

Rows 10-129: Repeat Rows 4 and 5 for pattern, working in the following stripe sequence: ★ 10 Rows **each** of Color B, Color C, Color A; repeat from ★ 3 times **more**: 260 sts.

Bind off all sts in **knit**.

Short Row Scarf

SHOPPING LIST

Yarn (Medium Weight)

[3.5 ounces, 200 yards
(100 grams, 182 meters) per skein]:

☐ Color A (Grey) - 1 skein
☐ Color B (Sage) - 1 skein

Knitting Needles

☐ Straight, size 8 (5 mm)
   or size needed for gauge

GAUGE INFORMATION

In Garter Stitch,
   24 sts = 5" (12.75 cm),
   32 rows (2 Wedges) = 4¼" (10.75 cm)

Finished Size: 5" wide x 53" long (12.75 cm x 134.5 cm)

SHORT ROWS

Short rows are formed by working across only some of the stitches before stopping and working back. This method forms the wedges.

In order to prevent holes, it is necessary to wrap the yarn around an unworked stitch before changing directions.

To wrap a st before turning, slip the next stitch as if to **purl**, bring the yarn forward, slip the stitch back onto the left needle *(Fig. A)*.

Fig. A

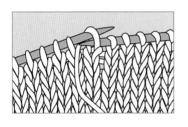

SCARF

With Color A, cast on 24 sts.

FIRST WEDGE

Row 1 (Right side)**:** With Color A, knit across.

Row 2: Knit across to last 4 sts, wrap next st; turn.

Row 3: Knit across.

Row 4: K 17, wrap next st; turn.

Row 5: Knit across.

Row 6: K 14, wrap next st; turn.

Row 7: Knit across.

Row 8: K 11, wrap next st; turn.

Row 9: Knit across.

Row 10: K8, wrap next st; turn.

Row 11: Knit across.

Row 12: K5, wrap next st; turn.

Row 13: Knit across.

Row 14: K2, wrap next st; turn.

Rows 15 and 16: Knit across.

Cut Color A.

SECOND WEDGE

Row 1 (Right side)**:** With Color B, K3, wrap next st; turn.

Row 2: Knit across.

Row 3: K6, wrap next st; turn.

Row 4: Knit across.

Row 5: K9, wrap next st; turn.

Row 6: Knit across.

Row 7: K 12, wrap next st; turn.

Row 8: Knit across.

Row 9: K 15, wrap next st; turn.

Row 10: Knit across.

Row 11: K 18, wrap next st; turn.

Row 12: Knit across.

Row 13: K 21, wrap next st; turn.

Rows 14-16: Knit across.

Cut Color B.

Repeat First and Second Wedges until Scarf measures approximately 53" (134.5 cm) from cast on edge, ending by working Second Wedge.

Bind off all sts in **knit**.

Striped Criss-Cross Scarf

SHOPPING LIST

Yarn (Medium Weight) 🔳**4**
- ☐ Color A (Rose) - 135 yards (123 meters)
- ☐ Color B (Metallic) - 120 yards (110 meters)

Knitting Needles
- ☐ Straight, size 9 (5.5 mm) **or** size needed for gauge

Additional Supplies
- ☐ Stitch holders - 2
- ☐ Yarn needle

GAUGE INFORMATION

In pattern,

20 sts = 5" (12.75 cm),

36 rows (3 repeats) = 5½" (14 cm)

TECHNIQUES USED

- YO *(Fig. 3a, page 42)*
- Knit increase *(Figs. 4a & b, page 43)*
- K2 tog *(Fig. 5, page 43)*

Finished Size: 5" wide x 55" long (12.75 cm x 139.5 cm)

FIRST HALF

With Color A, cast on 20 sts.

Rows 1 and 2: Knit across.

Carry unused color along edge, twisting unused color every two rows.

Row 3 (Right side)**:** With Color B, knit across.

Row 4: Purl across.

Rows 5 and 6: With Color A, knit across.

Row 7: With Color B, knit across.

Row 8: Purl across.

Rows 9 and 10: Repeat Rows 7 and 8.

Rows 11-14: With Color A, knit across.

Row 15: K1, (YO, K2 tog) across to last st, K1.

Rows 16-18: Knit across.

Rows 19-162: Repeat Rows 7-18, 12 times.

Cut Color A.

CRISS-CROSS SECTION
FIRST STRIP

Row 1: With Color B, K 10; slip remaining 10 sts onto st holder.

Row 2: K2 tog, knit across: 9 sts.

Row 3: K7, K2 tog: 8 sts.

Rows 4-28: Knit across.

Row 29 (Increase row)**:**
Knit across to last 2 sts, knit
increase, K1: 9 sts.

Row 30: Knit across.

Rows 31 and 32: Repeat
Rows 29 and 30: 10 sts.

Cut yarn, slip sts onto second
st holder.

SECOND STRIP

Row 1: Slip sts from first
st holder onto needle; knit
across.

Rows 2-32: Work same as first
strip; do **not** cut yarn.

SECOND HALF

Row 1: With Color A, knit
across second strip; slip sts
from st holder onto needle
placing it behind sts just
worked and knit across: 20 sts.

Rows 2-152: Working same
as First Half, work Rows 12-18;
then repeat Rows 7-18,
12 times.

Rows 153-158: Repeat
Rows 7-12.

Row 159: With Color B, knit
across.

Row 160: Purl across.

Rows 161-163: With Color A,
knit across.

Bind off all sts in **knit**.

Tack the strips together at
the center of the Criss-Cross
Section to keep it in place.

Nubby Cowl

SHOPPING LIST

Yarn (Medium Weight) 🔴4🔴

- ☐ Color A (Grey) - 100 yards (91.5 meters)
- ☐ Color B (Blue) - 100 yards (91.5 meters)

Knitting Needle

- ☐ 24" (61 cm) Circular, size 9 (5.5 mm)
  or size needed for gauge

Additional Supplies

- ☐ Yarn needle

GAUGE INFORMATION

In Stockinette Stitch,
  16 sts and 28 rows = 4" (10 cm)

TECHNIQUES USED

- YO *(Figs. 3a & b, page 42)*
- K2 tog *(Fig. 5, page 43)*
- P3 tog *(Fig. 7, page 44)*

Finished Size: 30" circumference x 7" high (76 cm x 18 cm)

COWL

With Color A and leaving a long end for sewing, cast on 122 sts; do **not** join.

Rows 1 and 2: Knit across.

Carry unused color along edge, twisting unused color every two rows.

Row 3 (Right side)**:** With Color B, K1, (YO, K2 tog) across to last st, K1.

Row 4: Purl across.

Row 5: K2, (YO, K2 tog) across to last 2 sts, K2.

Row 6: Purl across.

Rows 7 and 8: Repeat Rows 3 and 4.

Rows 9-11: With Color A, knit across.

Row 12: P1, ★ P3 tog keeping sts on left point, YO, purl same 3 sts tog slipping sts off left point; repeat from ★ across to last st, P1.

Row 13: With Color B, knit across.

Row 14: Purl across.

Row 15: With Color A, knit across.

Row 16: Repeat Row 12.

Row 17: With Color B, knit across.

Row 18: Purl across.

Rows 19 and 20: Repeat Rows 17 and 18.

Rows 21 and 22: With Color A, knit across.

Row 23: With Color B, K1, (YO, K2 tog) across to last st, K1.

Row 24: Purl across.

Row 25: K2, (YO, K2 tog) across to last 2 sts, K2.

Row 26: Purl across.

Rows 27-40: Repeat Rows 9-22.

Rows 41-48: Repeat Rows 3-10; at end of Row 46, cut Color B.

Bind off all sts in **knit**.

Weave end of rows together *(Fig. 9, page 45)*.

Textured Scarf

SHOPPING LIST

Yarn (Bulky Weight) 🧶**5**

[5.3 ounces, 312 yards
(150 grams, 285 meters) per skein]:

☐ 2 skeins

Knitting Needles

☐ Straight, size 9 (5.5 mm)
   or size needed for gauge

Additional Supplies

☐ Crochet hook (for fringe)

GAUGE INFORMATION

In Stockinette Stitch,
   18 sts = 4" (10 cm)

TECHNIQUES USED

• YO *(Fig. 3a, page 42)*
• K2 tog *(Fig. 5, page 43)*
• Slip 1 as if to **knit**, K2 tog, PSSO
   (Figs. 6a & b, page 44)

Finished Size: 7" wide x 62" long (18 cm x 157.5 cm)

SCARF

Cast on 32 sts.

Rows 1-4: Knit across.

Row 5 (Right side): K1, (YO, K2 tog) across to last st, K1.

Rows 6-9: Knit across.

Row 10: Purl across.

Row 11: (K1, P1) across.

Row 12: (P1, K1) across.

Rows 13-16: Repeat Rows 11 and 12 twice.

Row 17: Knit across.

Row 18: Purl across.

Rows 19-28: Repeat Rows 1-10.

Row 29: P1, K3, (P3, K3) across to last 4 sts, P4.

Row 30: K4, P3, (K3, P3) across to last st, K1.

Rows 31 and 32: Repeat Rows 29 and 30.

Row 33: K1, YO, slip 1 as if to **knit**, K2 tog, PSSO, YO, ★ K3, YO, slip 1 as if to **knit**, K2 tog, PSSO, YO; repeat from ★ across to last 4 sts, K4.

Row 34: Purl across.

Row 35: P4, K3, (P3, K3) across to last st, P1.

Row 36: K1, P3, (K3, P3) across to last 4 sts, K4.

Rows 37 and 38: Repeat Rows 35 and 36.

Row 39: K4, YO, slip 1 as if to **knit**, K2 tog, PSSO, YO, ★ K3, YO, slip 1 as if to **knit**, K2 tog, PSSO, YO; repeat from ★ across to last st, K1.

Row 40: Purl across.

Rows 41-52: Repeat Rows 29-40.

Rows 53-392: Repeat Rows 1-52, 6 times; then repeat Rows 1-28 once **more**.

Bind off all sts in **knit**.

Block Scarf lightly to 7" (18 cm) wide.

FRINGE

Cut a piece of cardboard 5" x 7" (12.5 cm x 18 cm). Wind the yarn loosely and evenly lengthwise around the cardboard until the card is filled, then cut across one end; repeat as needed.

Hold together 8 strands of yarn; fold in half.

With **wrong** side facing and using a crochet hook, draw the folded end up through a stitch and pull the loose ends through the folded end *(Fig. A)*; draw the knot up tightly *(Fig. B)*. Evenly space 7 fringes across each short end.

Lay flat on a hard surface and trim the ends.

Fig. A

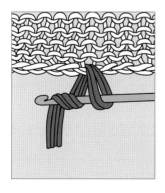

Fig. B

General Instructions

ABBREVIATIONS

cm	centimeters
K	knit
mm	millimeters
P	purl
Rnd(s)	Round(s)
st(s)	stitch(es)
PSSO	pass slipped stitch over
tog	together
YO	yarn over

SYMBOLS & TERMS

★ — work instructions following ★ as many **more** times as indicated in addition to the first time.

( ) or [ ] — work enclosed instructions **as many** times as specified by the number immediately following **or** contains explanatory remarks.

colon (:) — the number(s) given after a colon at the end of a row or round denote(s) the number of stitches you should have on that row or round.

KNIT TERMINOLOGY	
UNITED STATES	**INTERNATIONAL**
gauge =	tension
bind off =	cast off
yarn over (YO) =	yarn forward (yfwd) **or** yarn around needle (yrn)

◼◻◻◻ BEGINNER	Projects for first-time knitters using basic knit and purl stitches. Minimal shaping.
◼◼◻◻ EASY	Projects using basic stitches, repetitive stitch patterns, simple color changes, and simple shaping and finishing.
◼◼◼◻ INTERMEDIATE	Projects with a variety of stitches, such as basic cables and lace, simple intarsia, double-pointed needles and knitting in the round needle techniques, mid-level shaping and finishing.
◼◼◼◼ EXPERIENCED	Projects using advanced techniques and stitches, such as short rows, fair isle, more intricate intarsia, cables, lace patterns, and numerous color changes.

GAUGE

Exact gauge is essential for proper size. Before beginning your project, make a sample swatch in the yarn and needle specified in the individual instructions. After completing the swatch, measure it, counting your stitches and rows carefully. If your swatch is larger or smaller than specified, **make another, changing needle size to get the correct gauge.** Keep trying until you find the size needles that will give you the specified gauge.

KNITTING NEEDLES		
UNITED STATES	ENGLISH U.K.	METRIC (mm)
0	13	2
1	12	2.25
2	11	2.75
3	10	3.25
4	9	3.5
5	8	3.75
6	7	4
7	6	4.5
8	5	5
9	4	5.5
10	3	6
10 1/2	2	6.5
11	1	8
13	00	9
15	000	10
17	---	12.75
19	---	15
35	---	19
50	---	25

Yarn Weight Symbol & Names	LACE (0)	SUPER FINE (1)	FINE (2)	LIGHT (3)	MEDIUM (4)	BULKY (5)	SUPER BULKY (6)
Type of Yarns in Category	Fingering, size 10 crochet thread	Sock, Fingering, Baby	Sport, Baby	DK, Light Worsted	Worsted, Afghan, Aran	Chunky, Craft, Rug	Bulky, Roving
Knit Gauge Range* in Stockinette St to 4" (10 cm)	33-40** sts	27-32 sts	23-26 sts	21-24 sts	16-20 sts	12-15 sts	6-11 sts
Advised Needle Size Range	000-1	1 to 3	3 to 5	5 to 7	7 to 9	9 to 11	11 and larger

*GUIDELINES ONLY: The chart above reflects the most commonly used gauges and needle sizes for specific yarn categories.

** Lace weight yarns are usually knitted on larger needles to create lacy openwork patterns. Accordingly, a gauge range is difficult to determine. Always follow the gauge stated in your pattern.

MARKERS

As a convenience to you, we have used markers to mark the beginning of a round or to mark increases. Place markers as instructed. You may use purchased markers or tie a length of contrasting color yarn around the needle. When you reach a marker on each row or round, slip it from the left needle to the right needle; remove it when no longer needed.

CIRCULAR KNITTING

When the Cowl is worked in the round, you are going to work around on the outside of the circle, with the **right** side of the knitting facing you.

Using a circular needle, cast on all stitches as instructed. Untwist and straighten the stitches on the needle to be sure that the cast on ridge lays on the inside of the needle and never rolls around the needle.

Fig. 1

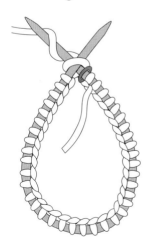

Hold the needle so that the ball of yarn is attached to the stitch closest to the right hand point. Place a marker on the right hand point to mark the beginning of the round.

To begin working in the round, knit the stitches on the left hand point *(Fig. 1)*. Continue working each round as instructed without turning the work.

ADDING STITCHES

Insert the right needle into the stitch as if to **knit**, yarn over and pull loop through *(Fig. 2a)*, insert left needle into loop just worked from **front** to **back** and slip it onto the left needle *(Fig. 2b)*. Repeat for the required number of stitches.

Fig. 2a

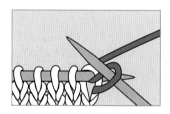

Fig. 2b

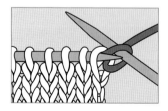

YARN OVER

Between two knit stitches

Bring the yarn forward **between** the needles, then back **over** the top of the right hand needle, so that it is now in position to knit the next stitch *(Fig. 3a)*.

Fig. 3a

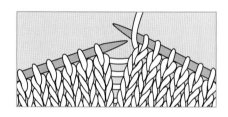

Between two purl stitches

Take the yarn over the right hand needle to the back, then forward under it, so that it is now in position to purl the next stitch *(Fig. 3b)*.

Fig. 3b

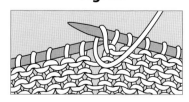

KNIT INCREASE

Knit the next stitch but do not slip the old stitch off the left needle *(Fig. 4a)*. Insert the right needle into the back loop of the same stitch and knit it *(Fig. 4b)*, then slip the old stitch off the left needle.

DECREASES
KNIT 2 TOGETHER

(abbreviated K2 tog)

Insert the right needle into the **front** of the first two stitches on the left needle as if to **knit** *(Fig. 5)*, then **knit** them together as if they were one stitch.

Fig. 4a

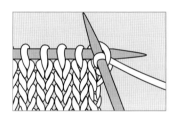

Fig. 5

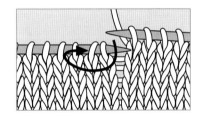

Fig. 4b

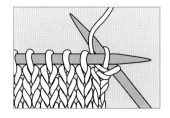

SLIP 1, KNIT 2 TOGETHER, PASS SLIPPED STITCH OVER

(abbreviated slip 1, K2 tog, PSSO)

Slip one stitch as if to knit *(Fig. 6a)*, then knit the next two stitches together *(Fig. 5, page 43)*. With the left needle, bring the slipped stitch over the stitch just made *(Fig. 6b)* and off the needle.

Fig. 6a

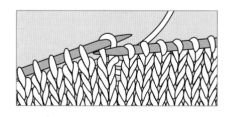

Fig. 6b

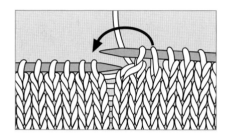

PURL 3 TOGETHER

(abbreviated P3 tog)

Insert the right needle into the **front** of the first three stitches on the left needle as if to **purl** *(Fig. 7)*, then **purl** them together as if they were one stitch.

Fig. 7

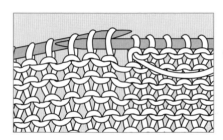

PICKING UP STITCHES

When instructed to pick up stitches, insert the needle from the **front** to the **back** under two strands at the edge of the worked piece *(Fig. 8)*. Put the yarn around the needle as if to knit, then bring the needle with the yarn back through the stitch to the right side, resulting in a stitch on the needle.

Repeat this along the edge, picking up the required number of stitches.

A crochet hook may be helpful to pull yarn through.

Fig. 8

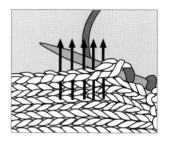

WEAVING SEAMS

With the **right** side of both pieces facing you and edges even, sew through both sides once to secure the beginning of the seam. Insert the needle under the bar between the first and second stitches on the row and pull the yarn through *(Fig. 9)*. Insert the needle under the next bar on the second side. Repeat from side to side, being careful to match rows.

Fig. 9

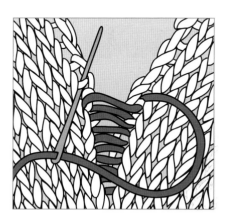

Yarn Information

The cowls and scarves in this book were made using a variety of yarns. Any brand of the specific weight of yarn may be used. It is best to refer to the yardage/meters when determining how many skeins or balls to purchase. Remember, to arrive at the finished size, it is the GAUGE/TENSION that is important, not the brand of yarn.

For your convenience, listed below are the yarns used to create our photography models. Because yarn manufacturers make frequent changes in their product lines, you may sometimes find it necessary to use a substitute yarn or to search for the discontinued product at alternate suppliers (locally or online).

GEOMETRIC STRIPED COWL
Lion Brand® Vanna's Style
Color A (Brown) - #125 Taupe
Color B (Salmon) - #134 Tomato
Color C (Ecru) - #098 Ecru

GARTER STRIPES COWL
Lion Brand® Heartland®
Color A (Ecru) - #098 Acadia
Lion Brand® Shawl in a Ball®
Color B (Metallic) - #302
   Metallic - Prism

LACE COWL
Patons® Lace™
#33008 Vintage

MOSAIC COWL
Premier® Yarns Deborah Norville Serenity® sock weight™
Color A (Off White) - #DN150-01 Soft White
Color B (Self-striping) - #DN104-07 Chili
Lion Brand® Vanna's Glamour®
Color C (Fuchsia Metallic) - #146 Jewel

TRIANGLE SCARF
Universal Yarn Whisper Lace
Color A (Blue) - #114 Lapis
Color B (Ecru) - #101 Mallow
Color C (Multi) - #213 Cool Ripples

SHORT ROW SCARF
Bernat® Satin™
Color A (Grey) - #04045 Grey Mist Heather
Color B (Sage) - #04232 Sage

STRIPED CRISS-CROSS SCARF
Lion Brand® Heartland®
Color A (Rose) - #103 Denali
Lion Brand® Shawl in a Ball®
Color B (Metallic) - #304 Metallic - Lotus Blossom

NUBBY COWL
Lion Brand® Jeans®
Color A (Grey) - #150Y Vintage
Color B (Blue) - #109W Stonewash

TEXTURED SCARF
Lion Brand® Scarfie
#206 Cream/Taupe

Meet Andi Javori

Andi Javori's goal as a designer is to inspire knitters and crocheters to be fearless. "I always recommend experimenting with different yarns and color combinations and to have fun with it," she says. "I like to utilize interesting yarn and color pairings, textured stitches, and other design elements such as fringe, bobbles, or ruffles to add a little sophistication and visual interest."

Growing up in Europe and around her grandfather's clothing boutique sparked her interest in fashion at an early age. "My love of knitting began at the age of 10, when my best friend's mother taught me how to knit, and I haven't stopped since. I then took it one step further and started experimenting with knitted jewelry and other beaded accessories."

More about Andi's patterns and kits for fashion accessories can be found on her website, JavoriDesigns.com. The full-time designer lives in New York with her husband, two sons, and a cat.

We have made every effort to ensure that these instructions are accurate and complete. We cannot, however, be responsible for human error, typographical mistakes, or variations in individual work.

Production Team: Writer/Technical Editor - Cathy Hardy; Editorial Writer – Susan Frantz Wiles; Senior Graphic Artist – Lora Puls; Graphic Artist - Kellie McAnulty; Photo Stylist - Lori Wenger; and Photographer - Jason Masters.